Beautiful Plants of the Bible
From the Hyssop to the Mighty Cedar Trees

Text & Photography by: **Dr. David Darom**

He spoke of trees, from the **cedar** that is in Lebanon to the **hyssop** that grows out of the wall.

I Kings 4:33

Printed by Israphot, Karney Shomron
Designed by F. Klevitsky

Produced by Palphot Ltd., P.O.Box 2, Herzlia 46100, Israel.
Tel. 052-555238, Telex: 33884, Fax: 052-571701.
ISBN 965-280-067-8

PUBLISHED BY PALPHOT. LTD

P r e f a c e

Plants are first mentioned in the Bible in the first chapter of the first book: "And God said, 'Let the earth put forth vegetations, plants yielding seed, and fruit trees bearing fruit in which is their seed, each according to its kind'" (Genesis 1:11) Throughout the ages, the Hebrews have attributed holiness to many species of plants. The Scriptures associate feasts, rites and commandments with many plants and their cultivation. Trees and woods were used as places of worship or were celebrated, with their fruit, in song and poetry to symbolize prosperity, beauty and peace. Field crops and vegetables were lacking in variety and man must have depended on the wild vegetation for much of his vegetable diet. Grass and herbs, on the other hand, flourished in the Land of Israel mainly because it is situated at the limit of the woodland and its herbaceous steppes are rich in annual and perennial edible plants. Hundreds of flowers cover Israel's mountains and valleys and even its deserts especially during springtime, but hardly any are mentioned in the Bible by a specific name. The overwhelming beauty of flowering meadows is often ascribed collective names, making it difficult to identify individual species that might have been referred to. Thus, more than 120 species of plants mentioned in the Bible present a fascinating study even though some have created perplexing problems in which botanists and theologists do not always see eye to eye. Most of these species of plants still grow in their wild state in the Holy Land although many of them have nowadays become extremely hard to find. All the photographs in this book have been taken in Israel, most of them depicting the wild species as they were known to our biblical ancestors. I have chosen about 80 species that present little or no difficulty in identification since they clearly refer to the plants of Bible times.

A LAND WHERE NOTHING IS LACKING

For forty years, the Children of Israel wandered around in the desert yearning to reach the Promised Land.

The desert is bare and dry, a land without water and without plants. But in the Promised Land, the Land of Canaan, fountains and deep waters flow from the valleys and mountains. It is a land with an abundance of rain and underground water, the cradle of ancient agriculture.

It is also the country of origin of the "Seven Species", wheat, barley, vine, fig, pomegranate, olive and date.

Here, in this region, at the edge of the "Fertile Crescent", the most ancient remains of wheat and barley (from about 10,000 years ago) were discovered. Here the first buds of agriculture sprouted.

The Scriptures do not simply say "olive" but "a Land of Olive trees" and not "date" but "honey", showing that man already knew these plants and how to extract their products – oil and honey.

However, also the stones and rocks of the Land are not simply "stones" and "rocks" but a Land whose stones are of iron and from whose mountains copper can be quarried. Indeed, the copper mines and iron of the Land of Israel were famous before the Children of Israel left Egypt.

The Promised Land is small but abounding with all that is necessary for man to put down roots, to flourish and bear fruit – water, vegetation and quarries.

WHEAT (Wheat)
Triticum durum

For the Lord your God is bringing you into a good land, a land of brooks of water, of fountains and springs, flowing forth in valleys and hills, a land of **wheat** and barley, of vines and fig trees and pomegranates, a land of olive trees and honey.

Deuteronomy 8:7–8

BARLEY (Barley)
Hordeum vulgare

So Naomi returned, and Ruth the Moabitess her daughter-in-law with her, who returned from the coutry of Moab. And they came to Bethlehem at the beginning of **barley** harvest.

Ruth 1:22

VINE (V
*Vitis vin

Behold, t
ing, says t
plowman
reaper a
grapes h
seed; the
drip swee
hills shall

POMEGRANATE
(Pomegranate)
Punica granatum

*And they came to the Valley of Eschol, and cut down from there a branch with a single cluster of grapes, and they carried it on a pole between two of them; they brought also some **pomegranates** and figs.*

Numbers 13:23

OLIVE (Olive)
Olea europaea

*The trees once went forth to anoint a king over them; and they said to the **olive tree**, 'Reign over us.' But the olive tree said to them, 'Shall I leave my fatness, by which gods and men are honoured, and go to sway over the trees?'*

Judges 9:8–9

DATE (Palm Tree)
Phoenix dactylifera

*The righteous flourish like the **palm tree**, and grow like a cedar in Lebanon. They are planted in the house of the Lord, they flourish in the courts of our God. They still bring forth fruit in old age, they are ever full of sap and green.*

Psalms 92:12–14

FIG (Fig)
Ficus carica

*For lo, the winter is past, the rain is over and gone. The flowers appear on the earth, the time of singing has come, and the voice of the turtledove is heard in our land. The **fig tree** puts forth its figs.*

Song of Solomon 2:11–13

s are com- , when the vertake the treader of sows the tains shall and all the h it.

Amos 9:13

HYSSOP (Syrian Hyssop)
Origanum syriacum

*He spoke of trees, from the cedar that is in Lebanon to the **Hyssop** that grows out of the wall.*

I Kings 4:33

The Syrian Hyssop grows abundantly in Israel and the Sinai desert among the dwarf shrubbery, usually on stony ground. Called **ezov** in Hebrew or **zaatar** in Arabic, it is used in tea and in cooked and baked food or as a popular spice eaten with bread and olive oil.

BITTER HERBS (Dwarf Chicory)
Cichorium pumilum

*They shall eat the flesh that night, roasted; with un-leavened bread and **bitter herbs** they shall eat it.*

Exodus 12:8

The Dwarf Chicory usually grows on roadsides and abandoned fields and under favorable conditions can reach a height of 1 m. It is sometimes used in salads or as a substitute for coffee.

PURSLANE (Mallow)
Malva sylvestris

*Can that which is tasteless be eaten without salt, or is there any taste in the slime of the **Purslane**? My appetite refuses to touch them.*

Job 6:6–7

A common pot-herb, the leaves of the Mallow are collected in early winter by peasants for soups and salads. The edible fruits resemble small round loaves giving the plant the native name **hubez**, meaning bread.

HERBS (Garden Rocket)
Eruca sativa

*One of them went out into the field to gather **herbs**, and found a wild vine and gathered from it his lap full of **wild gourds**, and came and cut them up into the pot of pottage, not knowing what they were... But while they were eating of the pot of pottage, they cried out, "O man of God, there is death in the pot!"*

II Kings 4:39–40

The garden rocket is an annual of the mustard family. It was formerly grown for its oil bearing seeds or as a substitute for pepper. Local villagers collect it as a pot-herb or for wild salad. The wild gourd's fruit is deadly poisonous but can be used in small portions for stomach pains. Both plants grow in the Jordan Valley.

GOURDS (Wild Gourd)
Citrullus cocoynthis

DESIRE (Caperbush)
Capparis spinosa

*They are afraid also of what is high, and terrors are in the way; the almond tree blossoms, the grasshopper drags itself along and **desire** fails; because man goes to his eternal home, and the mourners go about the streets.*
Ecclesiastes 12:5

This beautiful plant, with its large white flowers and fresh looking leaves is mentioned only once in the Bible, and even then using the word **avionah** ('desire'). In later writings such as the Talmud, **avionah** describes the fruit and flower buds of the caperbush. The Mishnah calls it **tzalaf** which is also its Hebrew name today.

The caperbush is a hardy and spiny shrub, flowering from March till August on the walls of Jerusalem and on cliffs around the Mediterranean.

The large flowers are in full blossom during the night, only to wither away at sunrise.

Flowers of the Field / Lilies

FLOWERS (Crown Daisy)
Chrysanthemum coronarium

FLOWERS (Common Poppy)
Papaver sp.

*And why are you anxious about clothing? Consider the **lilies of the field**, how they grow; they neither toil nor spin; yet I tell you, even Solomon in all his glory was not arrayed like one of these.*

Matthew 6:28–30

FLOWERS (Mountain Tulip)
Tulipa montana

*All flesh is grass, and all its beauty is like the **flower of the field**... The grass withers, the flower fades; but the word of our God will stand for ever.*

Isaiah 40:6,8

LILY (White Lily) *Lilium candidum*

*I am a rose of Sharon, a **lily** of the valleys. As a **lily** among brambles, so is my love among maidens.*

Song of Solomon 2:1–2

*The **flowers** appear on the earth, the time of singing has come, and the voice of the turtledove is heard in our land.*

Song of Solomon 2:12

LILY (Crown Anemone) *Anemone coronaria*

Most of the many flowering species of the Bible Land must have had specific names in biblical times, but since they have often been ascribed collective names they are not easy to distinguish. The first of spring flowers are the red anemones, tulips and poppies named **nitzanim** in the Song of Solomon 2:12 "The flowers (nitzanim) appear...". Also included in the term "flowers of the field" are the daisy-like flowers, bright colored and abundant throughout the Land. The white Lily is a probable candidate for the expression "Lily of the Valley" which indicates an extremely beautiful bloom.

ROSE (Wild Rose) *Rosa sp.*

*I grew tall like a palm tree in En-Gedi, and like **rose** plants in Jericho.*

Ecclesiasticus 24:14

Cultivation of roses began in the Mediterranean countries where the ancient inhabitants had a high regard for perfumes of which one of the earliest was rosewater. Four species of roses are native to Israel flowering in pinkish-white hues.

SAFFRON (Saffron Crocus) *Crocus sativus.*

*Your shoots are an orchard of pomegranates with all the choicest fruits... and **saffron**.*

Song of Solomon 4:13

Saffron is mentioned only once in the Bible, but later sources describe it as a plant whose flowers (the stigmas) were collected for healing purposes and as a yellow dye for food and beverages.

SHIKKERON (Henbane) *Hysoscyamus aureus*

*The boundary goes out to the shoulder of the hill north of Ekron, then the boundary bends round to **Shikkeron**, and passes along to Mount Baalah, and goes out to Jabneel.*

Joshua 15:11

The walls of old cities and rock crevices are the habitat of the Henbane. The plant contains a potent alkaloid that is also used as a narcotic substance in medicine.

MANDRAKE (Mandrake) *Mandragora autumnalis*

*In the days of wheat harvest Reuben went and found **mandrakes** in the field and brought them to his mother Leah. Then Rachel said to Leah, "Give me, I pray, some of your son's mandrakes". But she said to her, "It is a small matter that you have taken away my husband? Would you take away my son's mandrakes also?"*

Genesis 30:14–15

Since the early ages mandrakes were considered as aphrodisiacs and as an aid to barren women. Their strangely human-shaped roots are attributed with magical powers and prized by many.

The mandrake is a stemless perennial herb that in winter bears violet bell-shaped flowers on long stalks. The yellow-orange-plum shaped fruits remain in the field till early summer, their sweet scent floating far into the surroundings.

The **mandrakes** give forth fragrance, and over our doors are all choice fruits, new as well as old, which I have laid up for you, O my beloved.
Song of Solomon 7:13

My brother Reuben brought **mandrakes** from the field... and there were apples sweet scented growing above the water beds in the land of Aram.
Testaments of Issachar 1:3–5

PUAH (Dyers Madder) *Rubia tinctorium*

After Abimelech there arose to deliver Israel Topla the son of **Puah**, son of Dodo, a man of Issachar; and he lived at Shamir in the hill country of Ephraim.
Judges 10:1

Although the madder is mentioned in the Bible as a proper name it is often mentioned in post-biblical literature as a useful dyeing plant (producing a red dye) and as possessing virtuous properties.

GUM (Tragacanth) *Astragalus gummifer*

MYRRH (Ladanum) *Cistus incanus*

*Then they sat down to eat; and looking up they saw a caravan of Ishmaelites coming from Gilead, with their camels bearing **gum**, balm and **myrrh**, on their way to carry it down to Egypt.*

Genesis 37:25

*A little balm and a little honey, **gum**, **myrrh**, pistachio nuts, and almonds.*

Genesis 43:11

Some spices, like Gum and Myrrh were mixed together to form the sacred anointing oil and the fragrant incense used in the tabernacle. Both Gum and Myrrh are a gum substance exuded from a number of small shrubs.

WORMWOOD (White Wormwood)
Artemisia herba-alba

*Therefore thus says the Lord of hosts concerning the prophets: "Behold, I will feed them with **wormwood**, and give them poisoned water to drink."*

Jeremiah 23:15

There is no obvious contextual evidence that wormwood (Laanah in Hebrew) is a bitter plant. Yet its identification is supported by many commentators connecting it with the strongly aromatic and rather bitter desert shrub Artemisia.

GALL (Poison Hemlock) *Conium maculatum*

*And when they came to a place called Golgotha (which means the place of a skull), they offered him wine and drink, mingled with **gall**; but when he tasted it, he would not drink it.*

Matthew 27:33–34

In context Gall seems to denote a bitter and poisonous drink or food. The most obvious choice is the quite common Poison Hemlock that belongs to the Carrot family and flowers in spring near houses and in abandoned sites.

MINT (Mint) *Mentha longifolia*

DILL (Dill) *Anethum graveolens*

Dill is not threshed with a threshing sledge, nor is a cart wheel rolled over cummin.

Isaiah 28:27

DILL (Black Cummin) *Nigella sativa*

CUMMIN (Black Cummin) *Cuminum cyminum*

Woe to you, scribes and Pharisees, hypocrites! for your tithe mint and dill and cummin and have neglected the weightier matters of the law, justice and mercy and faith; these you ought to have done, without neglecting the others.

Matthew 23:23

All these spices grow wild in the Holyland, mint being the most common.

RUE (Common Rue) *Ruta chalepensis*

*But woe to you Pharisees! for you tithe mint and **rue** and every herb, and neglect justice and the love of God; these you ought to have done, without neglecting the others*
Luke 11:42

Rue is a small shrub native to the Mediterranean countries and is commonly grown in gardens for ornamental and medicinal purposes. The oil distilled from this plant has a distinct smell and is used as an antispasmodic and for several home remedies.

CORIANDER (Coriander) *Coriandrum sativum*

*Now the house of Israel called its name manna; it was like **coriander** seed, white, and the taste of it was like wafers made with honey.*
Exodus 16:31

The wild Coriander is an annual herb commonly occurring in Israel among winter crops. Belonging to the Carrot family, it was once widely cultivated as a condiment while its aromatic leaves were used to flavor food.

MUSTARD (Black Mustard) *Brassica nigra*

And he said, "With what can we compare the kingdom of God, or what parable shall we use for it? It is like a grain of **mustard seed**, *which, when sown upon the ground, is the smallest of all the seeds on earth; yet when it is sown it grows up and becomes the greatest of all shrubs, and puts forth large branches, so that the birds of the air can make nests in its shades".*

Mark 4:30–32

The wild mustard was extensively cultivated in biblical times as the source of mustard-seed oil and a medicament. It is a tall annual herb that grows around the Sea of Galilee.

PROVENDER (Chick Pea) *Cicer arietinum*

And the oxen and the asses that till the ground will eat salted **provender**, *which has been winnowed with shovel and fork.*

Isaiah 30:24

BEANS (Broad Bean) *Vicia faba*

*When David came to Maha-naim, Shobi the son of Nahash from Rabbah of the Ammo-nites... brought beds, basins, and earthen vessels, wheat, barley, meal, parched grain, **beans** and lentils, honey and curds and sheep and cheese from the herd, for David and the people with him to eat.*

II Samuel 17:27–29

*Then Jacob gave Esau bread and pottage of **lentils**, and he ate and drank, and rose and went his way.*

Genesis 25:34

LENTILS (Lentil) *Lens culinaris*

*And you, take wheat and bar-ley, beans and **lentils**, millet and spelt, and put them into a single vessel, and make bread of them.*

Ezekiel 4:9

All three pulses mentioned in the Bible were widely cultivated by Early Neolithic farmers dating back to about 7000 BC. The broad bean and the chick pea are still an important part of the diet in all Middle Eastern countries.

LEEK (Leek) *Allium porrum*

We remember the fish we ate in Egypt for nothing, the cucumbers, the melons, the **leeks,** *the* **onions,** *and the* **garlic;** *but now our strength is dried up, and there is nothing at all but this manna to look at.*

Numbers 11:5—6

ONION (Onion) *Allium cepa*

GARLIC (Garlic) *Allium sativum*

Of these three common vegetables only the Garlic is of East Mediterranean origin. The Onion and Leek originated in Central Asia, but all were cultivated in Egypt and the land of the Bible since 3000 BC.

MELON (Watermelon) *Citrullus lanatus*

We remember the fish we ate in Egypt for nothing, the cucumbers, the **melons**, the leeks, the onions, and the garlic; but now our strength is dried up, and there is nothing at all but this manna to look at.

Numbers 11:5–6

The watermelon has been widely cultivated in most warm climates and was known in Egypt before the Bronze Age.

FLAX (Flax) *Linum usitatissimum*

The **flax** and the barley were ruined, for the barley was in the ear and the flax was in the bud.

Exodus 9:31

Spinning the fiber of flax produces linen, and its cultivation dates back to 5000 BC in the Land of Israel. Cotton was cultivated in India and Pakistan and also in America from at least 4500 BC. The cultivation of cotton in Israel began in the last centuries BC reducing the importance of flax.

COTTON (Cotton) *Gossypium herbaceum*

And when these days were completed, the king gave for all the people present in Susa the capital, both great and small, a banquet lasting for seven days, in the court of the garden of the king's palace. There were white **cotton** curtains and blue hangings caught up with cords of fine linen and purple to silver rings and marble pillars, and also couches of gold and silver on a mosaic pavement of prophyry, marble, mother-of-pearl and precious stones.

Esther 1:5–6

MILLET (Sorgum) *Sorgum bicolor*

And you, take wheat and barley, beans and lentils, **millet** and spelt, and put them into a single vessel, and make bread of them. During the number of days that you lie upon your side, three hundred and ninety days, you shall eat it.

Ezekiel 4:9

The whitish grains produced by the Sorgum plant are used to feed live-stock or for producing a crude type of bread. Sorgum grows in summer and the crop has to be irrigated where rainfall comes only in winter.

RUSH (Lake Rush) *Scirpus lacustris*

*And its canals will become foul, and the branches of Egypt's Nile will diminish and dry up, reeds and **rushes** will rot away.*

Isaiah 19:6

REED (Reed) *Phragmites australis*

*The Lord will smite Israel, as a **reed** is shaken in the water.*
I Kings 14:15

*And plaiting a crown of thorns they put it on his head, and put a **reed** in his right hand.*
Matthew 27:29

REED (Cattail) *Typha sp.*

*And when she could hide him no longer she took for him a basket made of **bulrushes**, and daubed it with bitumen and pitch; and she put the child in it and placed it among the **reeds** at ther river's brink. And his sister stood at a distance, to know what would be done to him. Now the daughter of Pharaoh came down to bathe at the river, and her maidens walked beside the river; she saw the basket among the **reeds** and sent her maid to fetch it.*

Exodux 2:3

PAPYRUS (Papyrus) *Cyperus papyrus*

*Can **papyrus** grow where there is no marsh? Can **reeds** flourish where there is no water?*

Job 8:11

*Ah, land of whirring wings which is beyond the rivers of Ethiopia; which sends ambassadors by the Nile, in vessels of **papyrus** upon the waters!*

Isaiah 18:1–2

The Reed, Cattail and Papyrus were commonly used in everyday life for making flutes, pens, walking canes, as material for house building, foremats, basketwork and for manufacturing boats, shoes and paper.

WEEDS (Darnel) *Lolium temulentum*

The kingdom of heaven may be compared to a man who sowed good seed in his filed; but while men were sleeping, his enemy came and sowed **weeds** *among the wheat, and went away.*

Matthew 13:24–25

The seeds of both Darnel and Scabiens are similar in shape and size to those of wheat. They mix and are difficult to separate, producing a poor flour, and also continue to grow with the new crop.

WEEDS (Scabiens) *Cephalaria syriaca*

NETTLES (Nettle) *Utrica pilulifera*

*Moab shall become like So-
dom, and the Ammonites like
Gomorrah, a land possessed
by **nettles** and salt pits, and a
waste for ever.*

Zephaniah 2:9

THORNS (Thorny burnet)
Sarcopoterium spinosum;

*__Thorns__ and snares are in the
way of the perverse; he who
guards himself will keep far
from them.*

Proverbs 22:5

THORNS (Christ Thorn) *Ziziphus spina-christi*

*Then the soldiers of the governor took Jesus into the praetorium, and they gathered the whole battalion before him. And they stripped him and put a scarlet robe upon him, and plaiting a crown of **thorns** they put it on his head, and put a reed in his right hand. And kneeling before him they mocked him, saying, "Hail, King of the Jews!"*

Matthew 27:27–29

While the generic terms apply to small spiny or prickly shrubs and vines, it seems quite possible that the text refers to specific species. All these quite common plants, numbering nearly 200 species in the Holy Land, form the low scrubby rabble of plant life that thrives along road sides and in neglected areas.

THORNS & BRIERS (Syrian Thistle)
Notobesis syriaca;

*Instead of the thorn shall come up the cypress; instead of the **brier** shall come up the myrtle; and it shall be to the Lord for a memorial, for an everlasting sign which shall not be cut off.*

Isaiah 15:13

THISTILE (Globe Thistle) *Echinops viscosus*

And to Adam he said, "Because you have listened to the voice of your wife, and have eaten of the tree of which I commanded you, 'You shall not eat of it,' cursed is the ground because of you; in toil you shall eat of it all the days of your life; thorns and **thistles** it shall bring forth to you."

Genesis 3:17–18

The high places of Aven, the sin of Israel, shall be destroyed. Thorn and **thistle** shall grow upon their altars.

Hosea 10:8

THISTILE (Thistle) *Centaurea iberica*

BRAMBLES (Golden Thistle) *Scolymus maculatus*

I am a rose of Sharon, a lily of the valleys. As a lily among **brambles**, *so is my love among maidens.*

Song of Solomon 2:1–2

For each tree is known by its own fruit. For figs are not gathered from thorns, nor are grapes picked from a **bramble bush**.

Luke 6:44

WHIRLING (Tournefort's Gundelia)
Gundelia tournefortii

O my God, make them like **whirling** *dust, like chaff before the wind.*

Psalms 83:13

The term Whirling (or Galgal in Hebrew) is not the plant's name but probably indicates the fact that when dry, this tumbleweed rolls with the wind and dust in the open plains of the Holy Land.

LYE (Hammada) *Hammada Salicornis*

Though you wash yourself with **lye** *and use much soap, the stain of your guilt is still before me, says the Lord God.*

Jeremiah 2:22

The different species of Hammada served since Biblical times for making soap. Mixed with certain ashes and olive oil it is still found in many markets of the Orient.

BROOM (White Broom) *Retama raetam*

*But he himself went a day's journey into the wilderness, and sat down under a **broom tree**; and he asked that he might die, saying, "It is enough; now, O Lord, take away my life; for I am not better than my fathers."*

I Kings 19:4

*Through want and hard hunger they gnaw the dry and desolate ground; they pick mallow and the leaves of bushes, and to warm themselves the roots of the **broom**.*

Job 30:3–4

The White Broom is a tall shrub common to the deserts of Israel and Arabia. It grows in sandy soil and stony hillsides providing good shade, while the roots, being long and thick, make excellent and abundant material for campfires.

BUSH (Senna Bush) *Cassia senna*

*Now when forty years had passed, an angel appeared to him in the wilderness of Mount Sinai, in a flame of fire in a **bush**.*

Acts 7:30

The most plausible identification of the burning bush is **Cassia senna**, a one meter high shrub that grows on the Sinai mountains and develops a rich bloom of large flowers "burning" in bright yellow hues.

MYRTLE (Common Myrtle) *Myrtus communis*

*Go out to the hills and bring branches of olive, wild olive, **myrtle**, palm, and other leafy trees to make booths, as it is written.*

Nehemiah 8:15

*I will put in the wilderness the cedar, the acacia, the **myrtle** and the olive; I will set in the desert the cypress, the plane and the pine together.*

Isaiah 41:19

An all-Mediterranean species, this evergreen shrub is one of the "four species" the Israelites were ordered to use on the first day of Tabernacles. Its aromatic branches have been put to many uses since biblical times and were used in many rituals by the ancient Greeks.

GOODLY TREES (Citron) *Citrus medica*

*And you shall take on the first day of the fruit of **goodly trees**, branches of palm trees, and boughs of leafy trees, and willows of the brook; and you shall rejoice before the Lord your God seven days.*

Leviticus 23:40

The Goodly Trees (Etz Hadar in Hebrew) are mentioned only once in connection with the "four species" of the Feast of Tabernacles. The **Citron** originated in India and was introduced into the Middle East during early biblical times.

ALMOND (Almond) *Amygdalus communis*

*And on the morrow Moses went into the tent of the testimony; and behold, the rod of Aaron for the house of Levi had sprouted and put forth buds, and produced blossoms, and it bore ripe **almonds**.*

Numbers 17:8

*They are afraid also of what is high, and terrors are in the way; the **almond tree** blossoms, the grasshopper drags itself along and desire fails; because man goes to his eternal home, and the mourners go about the streets.*

Ecclesiastes 12:5

NUT (Walnut) *Juglans regia*

*I went down to the **nut** orchard, to look at the blossoms of the valley, to see whether the vines had budded, whether the pomegranates were in bloom.*

Song of Solomon 6:11

PISTACHIO NUTS (Pistachio) *Pistacia vera*

*Then their father Israel said to them, "If it must be so, then do this: take some of the choice fruits of the land in your bags, and carry down to the man a present, a little balm and a little honey, gum, myrrh, **pistachio nuts**, and almonds."*

Genesis 43:11

Walnuts once grew in abundance in the Holy Land, while the **Pistachio** trees were introduced into the area from the East. The most common today, growing wild all over Israel, is the **Almond**. The wild almond is a bitter-seeded medium sized tree that sheds its leaves at the beginning of winter. Later, it is the first to sprout into magnificent pink and white blossoms – before leaf setting – at the end of a cold winter. The sweet seeded almond has been cultivated in the Holy Land for thousands of years, being grafted on the local wild bitter-seeded strains.

MULBERRIES (Black Mulberry) *Morus nigra*

*He who is **impoverished** chooses for an offering wood that will not rot; he seeks out a skilful craftsman to set up an image that will not move.*

Isaiah 40:20

*They showed the elephants the juice of grapes and **mulberries**, to arouse them for battle.*

I Maccabees 6:34

The **White Mulberry** and the **Black Mulberry** have been cultivated in the Land of the Bible for many centuries. The White Mulberry (introduced from China) was grown for its leaves on which the silk producing silk-worms were fed.

APPLE (Apple) *Malus sylvestris*

*Sustain me with raisins, refresh me with **apples**; for I am sick with love.*

Song of Solomon 2:5

*The vine withers, the fig tree languishes. Pomegranate, palm and **apple**, all the trees of the field are withered; and gladness fails from the sons of men.*

Joel 1:12

The **Apple** was probably introduced into Israel from Iran and Turkey as early as 4000 BC. Although it is commonly depicted throughout the ages as the forbidden fruit of the Garden of Eden, it is not in fact mentioned as such in the scriptures.

HENNA (Henna) *Lawsonia inermis*

*My beloved is to me a cluster of **henna** blossoms in the vineyard of En-Gedi.*

Song of Solomon 1:14

The **Henna** tree was grown mainly for its dye, which was produced from its dried leaves and applied to the nails, hair or used as a permanent cloth dye. The ancient Egyptians used **Henna** as a cosmetic; in India its fragrant flowers were used as offerings in rituals and it is still a common commodity in Arabian markets.

SYCAMORE (Sycamore) *Ficus Sycomorus*

*And he sought to see who Jesus was, but could not, on account of the crowd, because he was small of stature. So he ran on ahead and climbed up into a **sycamore tree** to see him, for he was to pass that way.*

Luke 19:3–4

The **Sycamore** in the Holy Land is an ancient relic of earlier tropical flora. This robust relative of the **Fig** produces figs much inferior in taste but its fruit was widely consumed by the poor. Its wood was used as excellent building timber being impervious to damp and rot.

PLANE (Laurestinus) *Viburnum tinus*

*I will put in the wilderness the cedar, the acacia, the myrtle, and the olive; I will set in the desert the cypress, the **plane** and the pine together*

Isaiah 41:19

The identification of the Hebrew equivalent of **Plane** (Tidhar) has failed so far. Later Aramaic translations render this plant as "Murran" or Laurestinus which is a low growing tree found in the forest of Carmel and widely cultivated for ornamental purposes.

WILLOW (Common Willow) *Salix acmophylla*

*And you shall take on the first day the fruit of goodly trees, branches of palm trees, and boughs of leafy trees, and **willows of the brook**; and you shall rejoice before the Lord your God seven days.*

Leviticus 23:40

*I will pour my Spirit upon your descendants, and my blessing on your offspring. They shall spring up like grass amid waters, like **willows** by flowing streams.*

Isaiah 44:3-4

The **willow** in these passages is one of the "Four Species" of the Feast of Tabernacles. The **willow** is common along fresh water streams in the Coastal Plain and the Jordan Valley.

POPLAR (White Poplar) *Populus alba*

*Then Jacob took fresh rods of **poplar** and almond and plane, and peeled white streaks in them, exposing the white of the rods.*

Genesis 30:37

The white **Poplar** is native to the Middle East and owes its name to its whitish bark. It is abundant in damp places and along riverbanks and is also grown for ornamental purposes as its whiteness stands out in decorative beauty against the landscape.

WILLOW (Euphrates Poplar) *Populus euphratica*

*By the waters of Babylon, there we sat down and wept, when we remembered Zion. On the **willows** there we hung up our lyres. For there our captors required of us songs, and our tormentors, mirth, saying, "sing us one of the songs of Zion!"*

Psalms 137:1–3

The **Euphrates Poplar**, which grows abundantly in the riverine Euphrates vegetation, is also found in the dense forest of the Jordan River bank. This river plant caused much confusion with the **Common Willow** as to the true identification of one of the "four species" to be taken at the Feast of Tabernacles.

PLANE (Oriental Plane) *Platanus orientalis*

*I grew tall like a palm tree in En-gedi, and like rose plants in Jericho; like a beautiful olive tree in the field, and like a **plane tree** I grew tall.*

Ecclesiasticus 24:14

The **Oriental Plane** grows tall (20 m.) and conspicuous in the riverine forest of northern Israel. It is easily identified by its 3–5 lobed hairy leaves that turn yellow-brown in Autumn.

ACACIA (Common Acacia) *Acacia raddiana*

*And you shall make upright frames for the tabernacle of **accacia wood**.*

Exodus 26:15

*And Joshua the son of Nun sent two men secretly from **Shittim** as spies, saying, "Go, view the land, especially Jericho."*

Joshua 2:1

The **Common Acacia** is most abundant in the desert where the Israelites wandered for forty years, and was therefore the most suitable species to produce wood for constructing the Tabernacle.

TAMARISK (Leafless Tamarisk) *Tamarisk aphylla*

*Abraham planted a **tamarisk tree** in Beer-Sheba, and called there on the name of the Lord, the Everlasting God.*
Genesis 21:33

*And they took their bones and buried them under the **tamarisk tree** in Jabesh, and fasted seven days.*
I Samuel 31:13

Several species of **Tamarisk** trees are scattered all over the sandy areas of the Israeli desert and in marshy areas and swamps. Their shade is a blessing and their soft branches are used as food for the sheep.

OAK (Terebinth) *Pistacia atlantica*

*And Joshua wrote these words in the book of the law of God; and he took a great stone, and set it up there under the **oak** in the sanctuary of the Lord.*
Joshua 24:26

Terebinth trees served as sites for worship and a burying places for the respected dead. The biblical name **elah** stems from the Hebrew **el** (god) and is usually associated with strength and sturdiness. Pistacia atlantica are among the most aged trees found in the Negev and Lower Galilee, and their dominating appearance is connected with several biblical stories.

OAK (Oak) *Querqcus ithaburensis*

And Deborah, Rebekah's nurse, died, and she was buried under an **oak** *below Bethel; so the name of it was called Allon-bacuth.*

Genesis 35:8

The Tabor oak, being a large deciduous tree that dominates its surroundings, was often associated with ritual and religious customs. Tabor oak forests once covered large areas of the northern Coastal Plain, the Lower Galilee, the Hulah Valley and the slopes of the Golan. Most of the trees were cut down during the ages so their excellent wood could be used in buildings, furniture and boats.

Yet I destroyed the Amorite before them, whose height was like the height of the cedars, and who was as strong as the **oaks**.

Amos 2:9

FIR TREES (Cypress) *Cupresus sempervirens*

And Hiram King of Tyre had supplied Solomon with cedar and **cypress** timber and gold, as much as he desired.

I Kings 9:11

O Tyre, you have said, "I am perfect in beauty." Your borders are in the heart of the seas; your builders made perfect your beauty. They made all your planks of **fir trees** from Senir.

Ezekiel 27:5

The **Cypress** was once common in the Judean mountains and its wood was often used for building and furniture. The **Cypress** is an evergreen coniferous tree that grows tall and conspicuous in the surrounding woods.

CEDAR (Cedar) *Cedrus libani*

Photo: Dr. A. Shmida

And Solomon sent work to Hiram the king of Tyre: "As you dealt with David my father and sent him **cedar** to build himself a house to dwell in, so deal with me... Send me also cedar, cypress, and algum timber from Lebanon, for I know that your servants know how to cut timber in Lebanon."

II Chronicles 2:3, 8

Because of its superior quality, fragrance and durability, the **Cedar** symbolizes strength, dignity and grandeur. Both the First and the Second Temples in Jerusalem were constructed of cedar wood.

Beautiful Plants of The Bible
From The Hyssop to The Mighty Cedar Trees

THE 'SEVEN SPECIES'

Wheat, Barley, Vine, Fig, Pomegranate, Olive and Date .... Deuteronomy 8:7–8
HYSSOP (Syrian Hyssop) *Origanum syriacum* .... Exodus 12:21–22, John 19:28–30
PURSLANE (Mallow) *Malva sylvestris* .... Job 6:6–7
BITTER HERBS (Dwarf Chicory) *Cichorium pumilum* .... Exodus 12:8
HERBS (Garden Rocket) *Eruca Sativa* .... II Kings 4:39–40
GOURDS (Wild Gourd) *Citrullus cococynthis* .... II Kings 4:39–40
DESIRE (Caperbush) *Capparis spinosa* .... Ecclesiastes 12:5
FLOWERS (Common Poppy) *Papaver sp.,* .... Matthew 6:28–30
FLOWERS ((Crown Daisy)) *(Chrysanthemum coronarium* .... Isaiah 40:6
FLOWERS (Mountain Tulip) *Tulipa montana* .... Song of Solomon 2:12
LILY (White Lily) *Lilium candidum* .... Song of Solomon 2:1–2
LILY (Crown Anemone) *Anemone coronaria* .... Matthew 6:28–30
ROSE (Wild Rose) *Rosa sp.* .... Ecclesiasticus 24:14
SAFFRON (Saffron Crocus) *Crocus sattivus* .... Song of Solomon 4:13–14
SHIKKERON (Henbane) *Hyoscyamus aureus* .... Joshua 15:11
MANDRAKE (Mandrake) *Mandragora autumnalis* .... Genesis 30:14–15
PUAH (Dyers Madder) *Rubia tinctorum* .... Judges 10:1
GUM (Tragacanth) *Astragalus gummifer* .... Genesis 37:25
MYRRH (Ladanum) *Cistus incanus* .... Genesis 43:11
WORMWOOD (('White Wormwood) *Artemisia herba-alba* .... Jeremiah 23:15
GALL (Poison Hemlock) *Conium maculatum* .... Lamentations 3:19–20
MINT (Mint) *Mentha longifolia* .... Matthew 23:23
DILL (Dill) *Anethum graveolens* .... Matthew 23:23
DILL (Black Cummin) *Nigella sativa* .... Isaiah 28:27
CUMMIN (Cummin) *Cuminum cyminum* .... Matthew 23:23
RUE (Common Rue) *Ruta chalepensis* .... Luke 11:42
CORIANDER (Coriander) *Coriandrum sativum* .... Exodus 16:31
MUSTARD (Black Mustard) *Brassica nigra* .... Mark 4:30–32
PROVENDER (Chick Pea) *Cicer arietinum* .... Isaiah 30:24
BEANS (Broad Beans) *Vicia faba* .... II Samuel 17:27–29
LENTILS (Lentil) *Lens culinaris* .... Genesis 25:34
MELONS (Watermelon) *Citrullus lanatus* .... Numbers 11:5–6
LEEKS (Leek) *Allium porrum* .... Numbers 11:5–6
ONIONS (Onion) *Allium cepa* .... Numbers 11:5–6
GARLIC (Garlic) *Allium sativum* .... Numbers 11:5–6
FLAX (Flax) *Linum usitaissimum* .... Exodus 9:31
COTTON (Cotton) *Gossypium herbaceum* .... Esther 1:5–6

MILLET (Sorgum) *Sorgum bicolor*	....	Ezekiel 4:9
RUSH (Lake Rush) *Scripus lacustris*	....	Isaiah 58:5
REED (Reed) *Phragmites australis*	....	I Kings 14:15, Matthew 27:29
REED (Cattail) *Typha sp.*	....	Exodus 2:3
PAPYRUS (Papyrus) *Cyperus papyrus*	....	Job 8:11
WEEDS (Darnel) *Lolium temulentum*	....	Matthew 13:24–25
WEEDS (Scabiens) *Cephalaria syriaca*	....	Matthew 13:24–25
NETTLES (Nettle) *Utrica pilulifera*	....	Zephaniah 2:9
THORNS (Thorny burnet) *Sarcopoterium spinosum*	....	Hosea 2:6
THORNS (Christ Thorn) *Ziziphus spina-christi*	....	Matthew 27:27–29
THORNS & BRIERS (Syrian Thistle) *Notobesis syriaca*	....	Judges 8:7
THORNS & BRIERS (Globe Thistle) *Echinops viscosus*	....	Judges 8:7
THISTLE (Thistle) *Centaurea iberica*	....	Hosea 10:8
BRAMBLES (Golden Thistle) *Scolymus maculatus*	....	Song of Solomon 2:1–2
WHIRLING (Tournefort's Gundelia) *Gundelia tournefortii*	....	Psalms 83:13
LYE (Hammada) *Hammada salicornis*	....	Jeremiah 2:22
BROOM (White Broom) *Retama raetam*	....	I Kings 19:4
BUSH (Senna Bush) *Cassia senna*	....	Exodus 3:2–4
MYRTLE (Common Myrtle) *Myrtus communis*	....	Isaiah 41:19
CITRON (Goodly Trees, Citron) *Citrus medica*	....	Leviticus 23:40
ALMOND (Almond) *Amygdalus communis*	....	Numbers 17:8
NUT (Walnut) *Juglans regia*	....	Song of Solomon 6:11
PISTACHIO NUTS (Pistachio) *Pistacia vera*	....	Genesis 43:11
MULBERRIES (Black Mulbeery) *Morus nigra*	....	I Maccabees 6:34
APPLES (Apple) *Malus sylvestris*	....	Song of Solomon 2:5
HENNA (Henna) *Lawsonia inermis*	....	Song of Solomon 1:4
SYCAMORE (Sycamore) *Ficus Sycomorus*	....	Isahia 9:10
PLANE (Laurestinus) *Viburnum tinus*	....	Isaiah 41:19
WILLOW (Common willow) *Salix acmophylla*	....	Leviticus 23:40
POPLAR (White Poplar) *Populus alba*	....	Genesis 30:37
WILLOW (Euphrates Poplar) *Populus euphratica*	....	Psalms 137:1–3
PLANE (Oriental Plane) *Planatus orientalis*	....	Ecclesiasticus 24:14
ACACIA (Common Acacia) *Acacia raddiana*	....	Exodus 26:15
TAMARISK (Leafless Tamarisk) *Tamarisk aphylla*	....	Genesis 21:33
TEREBINTH (Oak) *Pistacia atlantica*	....	Joshua 24:26
OAK (Oak) *Quercus ithaburensis*	....	Amos 2:9
FIR TREES (Evergreen Cypress) *Cupresus sempervirens*	....	Ezekiel 27:3–5
CEDAR (Cedar) *Cedrus libani*	....	II Chronicles 2:3, 8